# Attainment's

# Survival GUIDE

## PERSONAL CARE

**MEN**

**Don Bastian**
**Tom Kinney**
**Autumn Garza**

# Survival Guide to Personal Care for Men

By Don Bastian, Tom Kinney, and Autumn Garza

Edited by Tom Kinney
Graphic design by Sherry Pribbenow
Illustrations by Jo Reynolds, Beverly Sanders
Photography by David Nelson

An Attainment Company Publication
Printed in United States of America
ISBN: 1-57861-847-9

**Attainment Company, Inc.**
P.O. Box 930160
Verona, Wisconsin 53593-0160 USA
1-800-327-4269
www.AttainmentCompany.com

# Contents

# Contents

# Contents

# Contents

# INTRODUCTION

# Routine

**Routine – a sequence of actions you follow regularly**

A **routine** is a series of activities. An activity is

something you do, like brushing your teeth. A **routine** is

 **1**

when you do several activities together one after another.

An example of a **routine** would be to brush your teeth.

Use mouthwash. Shower. Shave. Apply deodorant and get

dressed.

## A suggested morning routine for men:

**1**

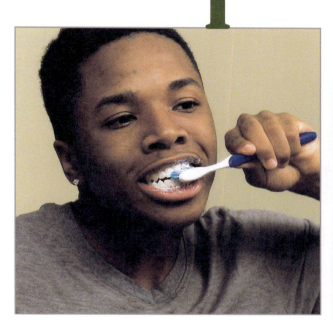

*Brush Your Teeth*

**2**

*Use Mouthwash*

**3**

*Take a Shower*

**4**

*Shave*

**5**

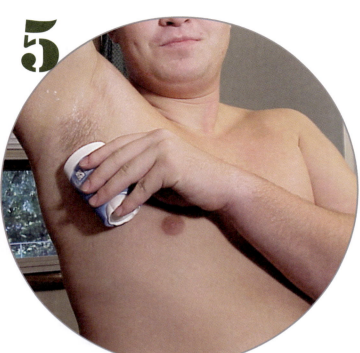

*Apply Deodorant*

**6**

*Get Dressed*

# CHAPTER 1

# Taking Care of Your Smile

Brushing Your Teeth

Flossing Your Teeth

Using a Water Pick

Using Mouthwash

Going to the Dentist

*Get your supplies ready for brushing your teeth and wet the toothbrush.*

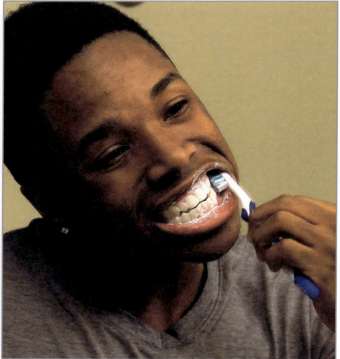

*Having clean-looking teeth is very important for first impressions.*

# Brushing Your Teeth

Toothpaste comes in many containers and brushes come in many styles.

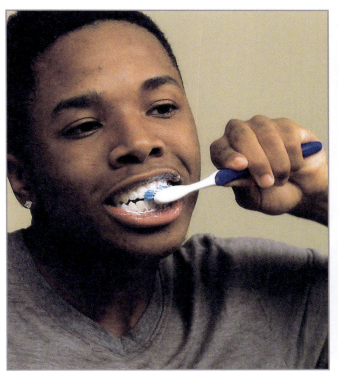

*Brushing your teeth carefully is important.*

# Vocabulary

| | | | |
|---|---|---|---|
| 1 | personal | | a person's private business |
| 2 | dental | | about your teeth |
| 3 | correct | A+ | the right way to do something |
| 4 | regular | | doing things in a consistent pattern |
| 5 | hygiene | | having good health practices |
| 6 | plaque | | bacteria on a tooth surface |

No **personal** care activity is more important than

good **dental** care. It is the key to fresh breath and

looking good. And it is important for health reasons. Brush

**2 3**

your teeth two or three times daily. But it is not enough

 **A+**

just to brush. It must be done **correctly**. Ask your dentist

to show you how to brush the right way.

# Step by Step

**1** *Get supplies.*

**2** *Wash hands.*

**3** *Wet toothbrush.*

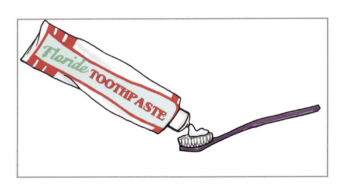

**4** *Apply toothpaste.*

**5** *Wet brush again.*

**6** *Brush teeth.*

**7** *Spit and brush more.*

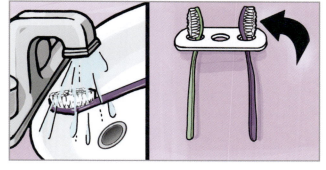

**8** *Rinse brush and put away.*

**9** *Fill up and rinse mouth.*

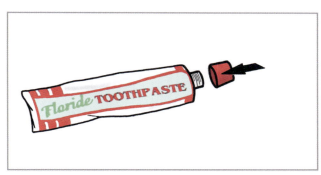

**10** *Put cap back on.*

**11** *Put supplies away.*

**12** *Brush your teeth after eating.*

See your dentist **regularly**. Ask your dentist to

give you an oral **hygiene** program for you to follow. And

ask your dentist for a **plaque** assessment to make sure

you are brushing properly. That will show if you need

to change the way you brush. Consider using an electric

toothbrush to stimulate your gums.

# Problem Solving

**1** You do not see your dentist often enough. What should you do?

_____

_____

_____

**2** You do not have a good oral hygiene program. What should you do?

_____

_____

_____

**3** You do not know if you are brushing correctly. What should you do?

_____

_____

_____

# Quiz

**1**  Keeping your teeth in good shape is called ____ care.

|  |  |  |
|---|---|---|
| dental | face | mouth |

**2**  Good dental care is important for _____ reasons.

|  | **3** |  |
|---|---|---|
| weather | three | health |

**3**  Make sure you _____ properly.

|  |  |  |
|---|---|---|
| eat | brush | dance |

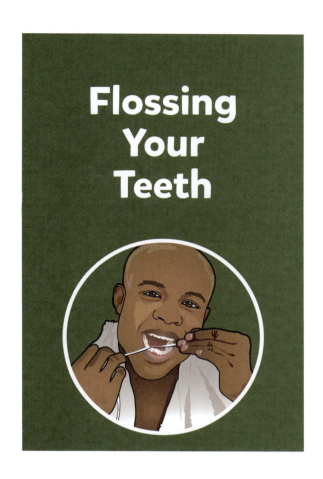

# Flossing Your Teeth

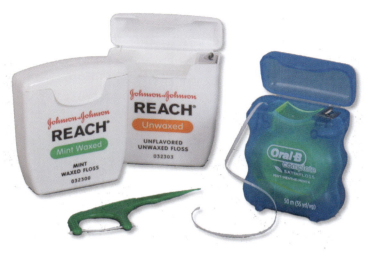

*There are different strengths of dental floss. Find what works for you.*

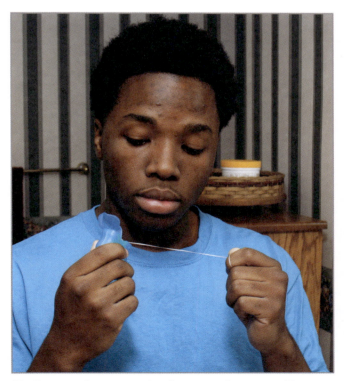

*Roll out about 18 inches and snap off.*

*Hold with both hands and insert between all teeth.*

# Vocabulary

| | | | |
|---|---|---|---|
| **1** | floss | | a soft thread used to clean between teeth |
| **2** | gum line | | where gums meet teeth |
| **3** | gums | | the pink tissue above your teeth |
| **4** | prefer | | to choose one thing over another |
| **5** | slide | | to move gently between two teeth when using dental floss |
| **6** | index finger | | the finger next to the thumb |

Flossing helps to remove plaque and food particles.

It allows you to clean your teeth in places a toothbrush

cannot reach. With dental **floss** you can clean under your

**gum line** and between your teeth. If possible, you should

try to floss at least once a day.

# Step by Step

**1** Get supplies.

**2** Wash hands.

**3** Roll out 18 inches of floss.

**4** Snap it off.

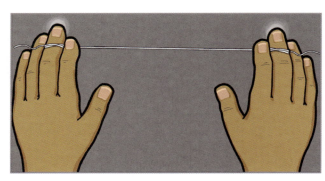

**5** Wrap floss around fingers.

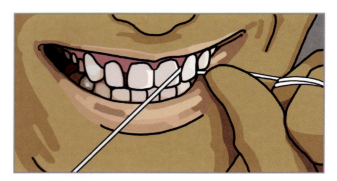

**6** Floss upper teeth.

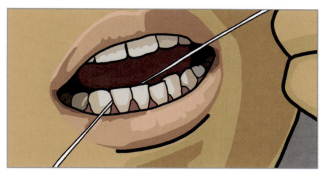

*Floss lower teeth.*

7

*Fill cup and rinse mouth.*

8

*Spit into sink.*

9

*Put floss away.*

10

Ask your dentist to show you how to floss

properly. Roll out 18 inches of **floss** and wind it around

the fingers you **prefer** to use. Usually the **index finger** or

 **2**

middle finger. Leave an inch or two between fingers to

floss with. **Slide** the floss down between each tooth until

you reach your **gums**, then slide it back up.

# Problem Solving

**1** You find flossing too difficult to do. What should you do then?

_____

_____

_____

**2** You often forget to floss. What can you do to remember?

_____

_____

_____

**3** Your dentist does not have time to show you how to floss. What should you do?

_____

_____

_____

# Quiz

**1**  Flossing helps to remove _____.

| hair | shoes | plaque |
|---|---|---|

**2**    Flossing helps you reach places a \_\_\_\_\_ cannot reach.

|  toothbrush |  pencil |  spoon |
|---|---|---|

**3**   With \_\_\_\_\_ \_\_\_\_\_ you can clean between your teeth.

|  orange juice |  dental floss |  watering can |
|---|---|---|

# Using a Water Pick

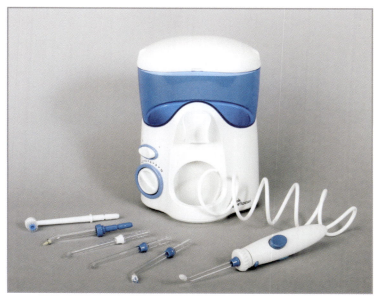

*If flossing is hard for you, try a water pick instead.*

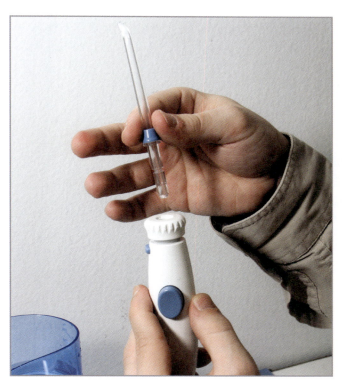

*Using a water pick is a good option.*

# Vocabulary

| | | | |
|---|---|---|---|
| 1 | option | | having choices to choose from |
| 2 | water pick | | a tool that uses a water jet to remove plaque and food debris |
| 3 | sensitive | | feeling pain easily |
| 4 | bacteria | | small organisms that can cause disease |
| 5 | comfortable | | feeling relaxed, at ease |
| 6 | decay | | to break down or rot |

Not everyone can floss their teeth. A great **option**

is to use a **water pick**. Water picks are also better for

those who have really **sensitive** teeth. Like flossing, a water

pick helps remove food deposits and plaque. It cuts down

on the **bacteria** that causes tooth **decay**.

# Step by Step

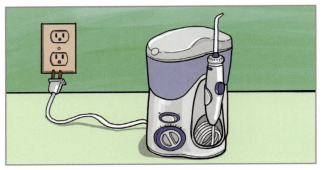

1. Plug in your water pick.

2. Fill the reservoir with lukewarm water.

3. Reset the reservoir on the base.

4. Select a tip and insert into the center of the probe at the top of the flosser handle. To remove a tip, press the eject button and pull up from the handle.

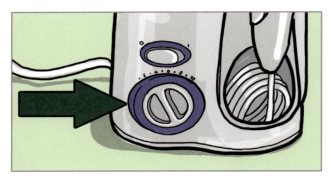

5. Turn the pressure control dial to the setting you prefer.

6. Lean over the sink and put the tip in your mouth.

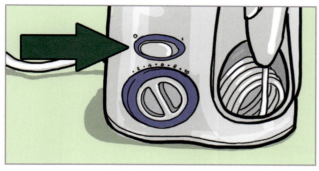

**7** With your free hand, turn on the water pick.

**8** Point the stream of water at your gums, letting the water fall into the sink.

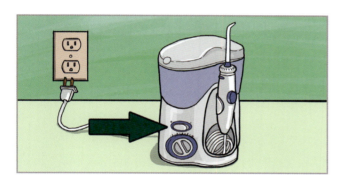

**9** When all the water is gone, turn off the water pick before you take it out of your mouth.

Use warm water in your **water pick**. It is more

**comfortable** for you and your teeth that way. Put enough

water in it so you do not have to refill in the middle

of cleaning. Ask your dentist to show you how to use it.

The more often you use your water pick, the easier it will

get.

# Problem Solving

**1** You find flossing to be too hard. What can you do?

_____

_____

_____

**2** You have sensitive teeth. What can you do?

_____

_____

_____

**3** You do not know how to use a water pick. What can you do?

_____

_____

_____

# Quiz

**1**  Not everyone can _____.

| | | |
|---|---|---|
|  spell | floss | sing |

**2**   An alternative to flossing is to use a _____ _____.

| | | |
|---|---|---|
| band aid | water pick | safety goggles |

**3** A water pick helps cut down on _____.

| | | |
|---|---|---|
|  bacteria |  grease |  wood |

# Using Mouthwash

*Types and sizes of mouthwashes.*

*Take a small amount of mouthwash in, swish around but don't swallow.*

# Vocabulary

| | | | |
|---|---|---|---|
| 1 | swish | | to force water around your mouth |
| 2 | force | | to make something happen |
| 3 | bad breath | | when your breath does not smell good |
| 4 | rinse | | to wash lightly with water |
| 5 | fluoride | | used in drinking water to prevent tooth decay |
| 6 | swallow | | to drink |

Mouthwash is a good way to get rid of

**bad breath**. **Swish** mouthwash with lips closed and teeth

# 30

apart. Continue for up to 30 seconds. Spit it out and

**rinse** your mouth with water. Wait 30 minutes before eating

or drinking after swishing. Take only a small amount of

**fluoride** mouthwash in your mouth and be careful not to

**swallow** it.

# Step by Step

**1** Get supplies.

**2** Remove lid.

**3** Pour in glass.

**4** Take a sip.

**5** Swish in mouth

**6** Spit in sink.

**7** *Rinse with water.*

**8** *Put supplies away.*

**9** *Be sure not to swallow.*

**10** *Don't drink out of bottle cap.*

**11** *Don't pour too much.*

Find the right mouthwash for you. Make an

appointment with your dentist if you have bleeding gums.

But you can also use a medicated mouthwash to treat

bleeding gums. Brush and floss before you **rinse** with

mouthwash. When you use mouthwash, **force** it around your

mouth so it reaches all areas.

# Problem Solving

**1** You do not know what kind of mouthwash to buy. What can you do?

_____

_____

_____

**2** You have bleeding gums. What should you do?

_____

_____

_____

**3** Your drinking water does not have fluoride. What can you do?

_____

_____

_____

# Quiz

**1**

Swish   mouthwash   into   all   corners   of   your   ____.

|  |  |  |
|---|---|---|
| hand | house | mouth |

**2**   **30**

Continue   swishing   the   mouthwash   for   30   ____.

| years | seconds | minutes |
|---|---|---|

**3**

Use   mouthwash   with   ____   if   your   drinking   water   lacks   it.

|  |  |  |
|---|---|---|
| soup | fluoride | fish |

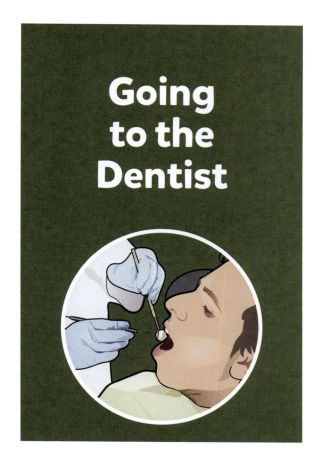

# Going to the Dentist

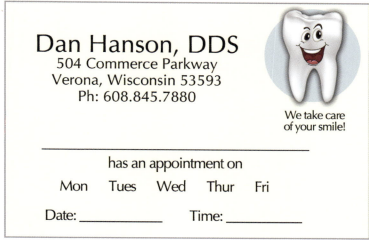

Dan Hanson, DDS
504 Commerce Parkway
Verona, Wisconsin 53593
Ph: 608.845.7880

We take care
of your smile!

_____

has an appointment on

Mon    Tues    Wed    Thur    Fri

Date: _____    Time: _____

*Make regular dental appointments.*

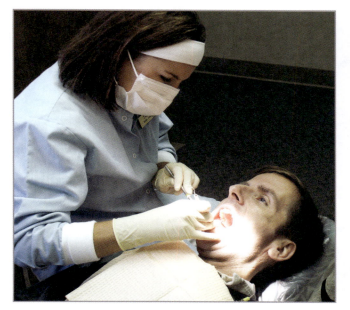

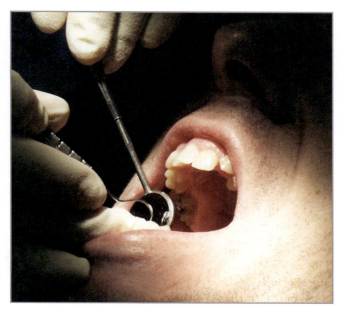

*With regular visits, your dentist will keep your teeth in good health.*

# Vocabulary

| | | | |
|---|---|---|---|
| 1 | dentist | | a person who takes care of your teeth |
| 2 | insurance card | ABC HEALTHCARE  NAME: JOHN DOE  POLICY #: 12345000 | a card that helps you pay your dental costs |
| 3 | relax | | to be at ease, not worried |
| 4 | nervous | | being too excited |
| 5 | question | **?** | to ask about something |
| 6 | explain | | to be clear about something |

See your **dentist** at least once or twice a year.

Make sure you brush and floss right before going to your

dentist. Take your dental **insurance card** with you. Try to

**relax**. Everyone gets **nervous** before seeing the dentist. Your

dentist may recommend that you get a fluoride treatment for

healthy teeth. Or a bleaching treatment to keep your teeth

white.

# Step by Step

**1** Check in with reception.

**2** Wait in waiting room.

**3** Go in when asked to.

**4** Sit in dentist's chair.

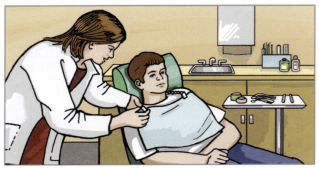

**5** The assistant will put a bib around you.

**6** Tell dentist your problem.

# Step by Step

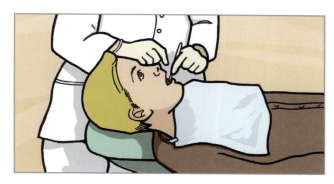

**7** *Dentist looks in your mouth.*

**8** *Dentist tells you what to do.*

**9** *Getting x-rayed.*

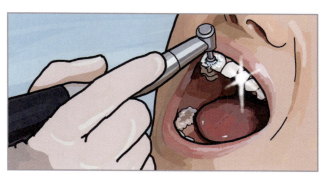

**10** *Cleaning your teeth.*

**11** *Thank dentist and assistant when you leave.*

**12** *Make another appointment on the way out.*

If you have **questions** for your **dentist**, write them

down before you go. Or have someone else write them

for you. If you don't know what the dentist is going to

do, just ask him to **explain**. If you are in pain, raise your

hand and tell her you need a break.

# Problem Solving

**1** You forget to make a dental appointment. What should you do?

_____

_____

_____

**2** You get nervous at the dentist's office. What can you do?

_____

_____

_____

**3** You are in pain. What can you do to get the dentist's attention?

_____

_____

_____

# Quiz

**1**  **2**

Go to your dentist at least once or twice a ____.

|  | | |
|---|---|---|
| month | year | day |

**2**

Brush and floss before you go to your ____.

|  |  |  |
|---|---|---|
| house | dentist | school |

**3**

Take your ____ ____ with you.

|  |  | |
|---|---|---|
| insurance card | dinner plate | white onion |

# CHAPTER 2

# Basic Personal Care

Taking a Shower

Taking a Bath

Shaving with an Electric Razor

Shaving with a Disposable Razor

Using Deodorant

*Make sure the temperature is right before getting in.*

*Don't forget to shampoo your hair . . .*

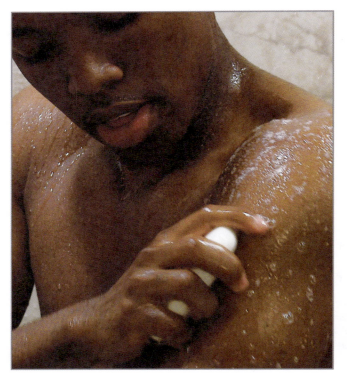

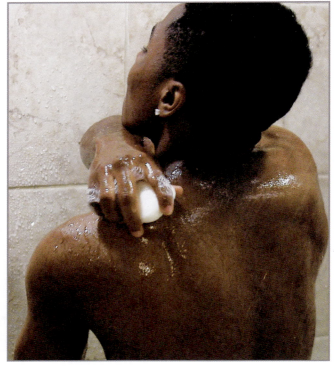

*. . . and carefully wash your entire body with soap.*

# Taking a Shower

Soaps come in many different forms.

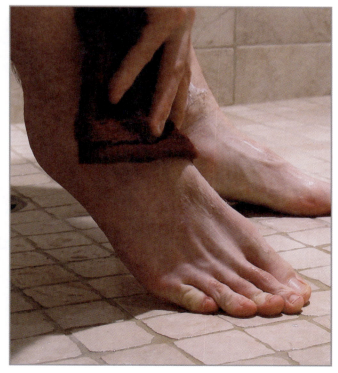

Taking a morning shower is an important part of your routine.

# Vocabulary

| | | | |
|---|---|---|---|
| 1 | shower | | to wash oneself in a shower stall |
| 2 | soap | | a cleansing agent to wash with |
| 3 | towel | | a cloth used for drying yourself |
| 4 | faucet | | a source of running water |
| 5 | temperature | | the degree of hotness or coldness |
| 6 | laundry | | clothes or linen that need washing |

To get ready for your day, start by taking a

**shower**. Make sure you have **soap** and shampoo at hand.

And a **towel** within reach of the shower. Do this before

you get in the shower. Turn the **faucet** or faucets to the

**temperature** you want before getting in. When you have

finished drying, put your towel somewhere it can dry off.

Or put it in the **laundry**.

**1**    *Get undressed.*

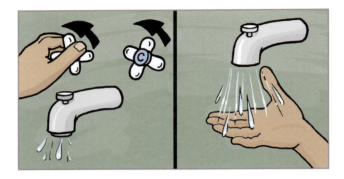

**2**    *Turn faucet to temperature you want.*

**3**    *Get in the shower.*

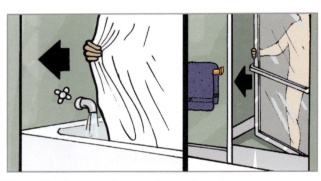

**4**    *Pull curtain or shut the door.*

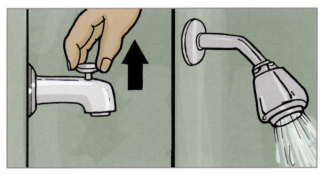

**5**    *Engage shower function (if necessary).*

**6**    *Get yourself wet.*

# Step by Step

**7** Lather soap for bubbles.

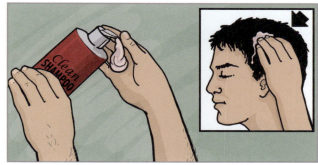

**8** Use shampoo for hair washing.

**9** Lather shampoo into scalp.

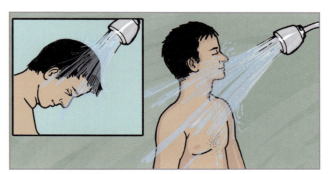

**10** Rinse off soap and shampoo.

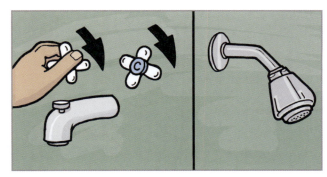

**11** Turn off faucet.

**12** Dry off.

# Helpful Tips

Turn on the **faucet** first and wait until it is warm

enough for you. Use your wrist to tell how warm it is.

Let the water cover all your body and your hair. Make

sure you rub the shampoo into your scalp evenly. Be

careful to rinse all the shampoo out of your hair. Rinse

the rest of your body carefully so you do not leave any

**soap** to dry.

# Problem Solving

**1** You are in the shower, but don't have any soap. What do you do?

_____

_____

_____

**2** You are all out of shampoo. What do you do?

_____

_____

_____

**3** You have trouble adjusting the temperature. What do you do?

_____

_____

_____

# Quiz

**1**  First  thing  in  the  morning,  take  a  _____.

walk

shower

cat

**2**  Make  sure  you  have  _____  before  getting  in.

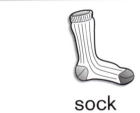

sock

soap

house

**3**  Turn  the  _____  to  the  _____  you  want.

faucet

temperature

mouse

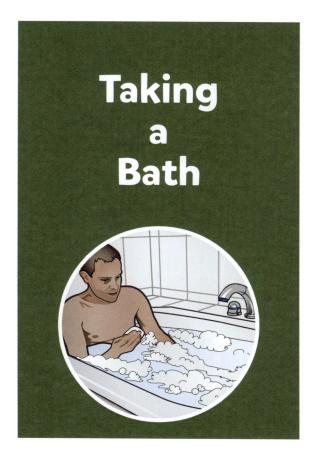

# Taking a Bath

Bath supplies include soap, sponges, brush, and a loofah.

Find the right temperature first, then clean with soap.

# Vocabulary

| 1 | bath | | a tub you lie or sit in to clean yourself |
| 2 | tub | | another name for a bath |
| 3 | shampoo | | a product used to wash hair |
| 4 | washcloth | | a small towel to wash your body with |
| 5 | lift | | to raise over |
| 6 | smooth | | a surface without bumps |

First make sure the bathroom is warm so you do

not get cold. To do so, turn on the faucet or faucets

and get the temperature you want. Make sure the door

is shut to keep the heat in. Get your supplies. Soap.

**Shampoo**. Conditioner. **Washcloth**. Towel. Be careful to **lift**

your legs over the **tub** getting in and out.

# Step by Step

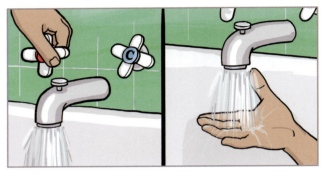

**1** Test the right temperature first before getting in.

**2** You can use bubbles or gel to make your bath more pleasant if you want.

**3** Get undressed while the bath fills.

**4** Get in and find a comfortable position.

**5** Lather your hands and body with soap.

**6** Wash your face and arms.

**7** *Apply shampoo.*

**8** *Lather shampoo into your scalp.*

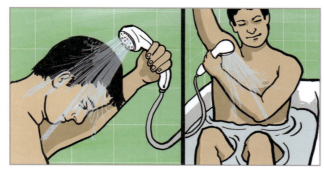

**9** *Rinse off shampoo and soap.*

**10** *Step out of tub. Be careful getting out.*

**11** *Dry off.*

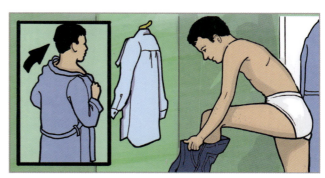

**12** *Get dressed.*

**Taking a Bath    67**

# Helpful Tips

Make sure your needed supplies are within your

reach of the **tub**. That way, you don't need to get out of

the **bath** to get them. Water that is too hot or too cold

will dry your skin. Draw a warm bath. You might put a

little baby oil in your bath to make your skin feel **smooth**.

# Problem Solving

**1** Your bathroom is always cold. What can you do?

_____

_____

_____

**2** You don't know where your supplies are. What should you do?

_____

_____

_____

**3** Your skin is often dry and uncomfortable. What should you do?

_____

_____

_____

# Quiz

**1**

Make sure the bathroom is warm so you don't get ____.

|  |  |  |
|:---:|:---:|:---:|
| old | sad | cold |

**2**

Turn on the faucet to get the ____ you want.

|  |  |  |
|:---:|:---:|:---:|
| sink | temperature | candy |

**3**

Get the ____ you need to take a bath.

|  |  |  |
|:---:|:---:|:---:|
| dog | supplies | cake |

# Shaving with an Electric Razor

*Supplies for shaving include electric razor and shaving lotions.*

*Shaving with an electric razor is easy once you learn how.*

# Vocabulary

| | | | |
|---|---|---|---|
| 1 | shave | | to cut off facial hair |
| 2 | rub | | to move along a surface |
| 3 | shaving lotion | | a liquid that makes it easier to shave |
| 4 | electric razor | | a tool to shave facial hair |
| 5 | screen | | a razor's protective guard |
| 6 | blades | | the part of the razor that cuts your facial hair |

Wash and dry your face before you start to

shave. **Rub** your hand over your face to see which way

your beard is growing. It may grow differently in different

places. **Shave** in front of a well-lit mirror so you can

clearly see what you are doing. It will save you time and

effort. And use a **shaving lotion** to make shaving easier.

# Step by Step

**1** Get shaving supplies.

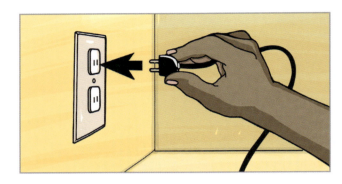

**2** Plug your electric razor in the wall socket.

**3** Shave in front of a mirror.

**4** Turn razor on.

**5** Start shaving on one side of your face.

**6** Look to see you didn't miss a spot.

**7** *Turn razor off.*

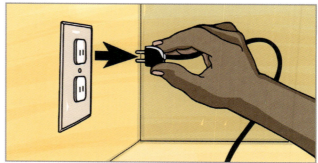

**8** *Unplug razor.*

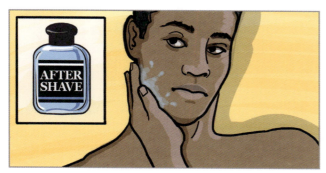

**9** *Put on after-shave.*

**10** *Put supplies away.*

# Helpful Tips

Clean your **electric razor screen** and **blades** every

third time you **shave**. Make sure you collect all your

shaving supplies before you start. Also, to give your

**electric razor** a clean surface to work with use a facial

cleanser before shaving.

# Problem Solving

**1** You do not have a well-lit mirror. What should you do?

_____

_____

_____

**2** You cannot tell which way your beard is growing. What should you do?

_____

_____

_____

**3** You do not understand how to clean your razor. What can you do?

_____

_____

_____

# Quiz

**1**

Wash and dry your face before you start to _____.

|  |  |  |
|:---:|:---:|:---:|
| sing | shave | sleep |

**2**

Rub a ____ over your face first.

|  |  |  |
|:---:|:---:|:---:|
| hand | monkey | banana |

**3**

Shave in front of a ____ to see better

|  |  |  |
|:---:|:---:|:---:|
| horse | car | mirror |

# Shaving with a Disposable Razor

*Supplies for disposable razor.*

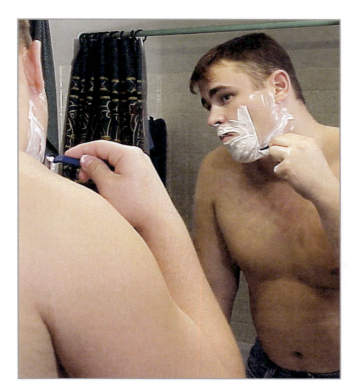

*Shave in front of a well-lit mirror.*

| | | | |
|---|---|---|---|
| 1 | shave | | the act of removing body hair |
| 2 | disposable razor | | a razor you use once and throw away |
| 3 | accident | | an event that happens by chance, not choice |
| 4 | mirror | | a piece of glass that reflects an image |
| 5 | baggy | | clothes that don't fit tight |
| 6 | supplies | | items needed to complete a task |

You need to be very careful when **shaving** with

a **disposable razor**. It is easy to cut yourself by **accident**.

Make sure you shave in front of a well-lit **mirror** to see

clearly what you're doing. Don't wear a **baggy** shirt, it

might get in your way. Collect all the **supplies** you need

before you start.

# Step by Step

**1** Turn on faucet.

**2** Wet your face.

**3** Spray shaving cream on your hand.

**4** Use a well-lit mirror.

**5** Rub shaving cream on face.

**6** Start shaving on one side of your face.

**7** *Rinse shaving cream off razor.*

**8** *Continue shaving.*

**9** *See if you missed any spots.*

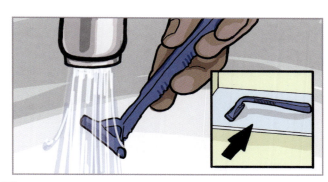

**10** *Rinse shaving cream off and put razor away.*

**11** *Use water to remove shaving cream from face.*

**12** *Dry face with towel.*

**Shaving with a Disposable Razor**    **83**

Gather your **supplies** and try to relax yourself.

**Shaving** with a **razor** requires being in a calm state. To

use shaving cream, hold the can with one hand and press

down on the release valve with the other. Spray the cream

on your hand and rub it on your facial hair. Shave with

a downward motion. When the razor fills with cream, rinse

it off.

# Problem Solving

**1** You are ready to start but find your razor is dull. What do you do?

_____

_____

_____

**2** You are concerned that you may cut yourself shaving. What do you do?

_____

_____

_____

**3** The shaving cream can doesn't seem to work. What do you do?

_____

_____

_____

# Quiz

**1**

Be careful when shaving with a _____.

|  |  |  |
|:---:|:---:|:---:|
| book | dog | razor |

**2**

Shave in front of a _____ mirror.

|  |  |  |
|:---:|:---:|:---:|
| blue | well-lit | old |

**3**

Collect all your _____ before starting.

|  |  |  |
|:---:|:---:|:---:|
| marbles | supplies | apples |

# Using Deodorant

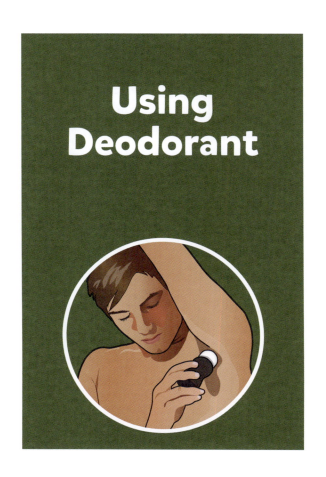

*Deodorant containers.*

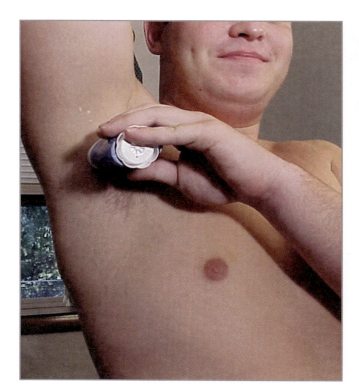

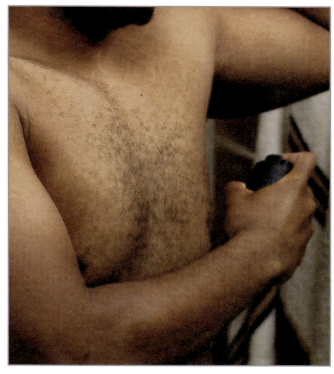

*Use deodorant to prevent body odor.*

# Vocabulary

| | | | |
|---|---|---|---|
| **1** | sweat | | when you perspire through skin pores |
| **2** | odor | | a bad smell |
| **3** | deodorant | | something you put on to prevent body odor |
| **4** | mask | | to cover something up |
| **5** | natural | | something present in nature |
| **6** | synthetic | Polyester | clothes not made from natural products |

Other people can smell our body **odors** when we

**sweat**. **Deodorants** help us hide our **natural** body odor.

Use a deodorant only after you have washed yourself.

Otherwise it will only **mask** the smell that is there. Make

sure to use your deodorant before you get dressed, or the

smell will carry over to your clothes.

# Step by Step

**1** *Finish your shower or bath.*

**2** *Get the deodorant out.*

**3** *Open the cap.*

**4** *Turn the base to roll the deodorant up.*

**5** *Apply to the underarms . . .*

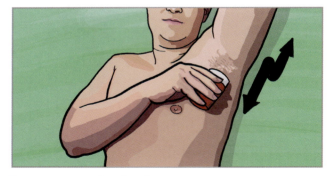

**6** *. . . under both arms.*

**7** *Replace the cap.*

**8** *Put deodorant back.*

**9** *Put on your shirt.*

Keep    enough    **deodorant**    around    so    you    do    not    run

out.    You    can    prevent    excess    **sweating**    several    ways.    Do    not

drink    too    much    coffee    or    eat    high-calorie    foods.    Consider

using    an    anti-perspirant    that    keeps    you    from    sweating.    Tight

fitting    or    **synthetic**    clothes    can    also    cause    you    to    sweat.

# Problem Solving

**1** You don't have any more deodorant. What do you do?

_____

_____

_____

**2** You put deodorant on this morning, but you are going out tonight. What do you do?

_____

_____

_____

**3** You forgot to put deodorant on this morning. What do you do?

_____

_____

_____

# Quiz

**1** When you sweat, others can smell your body _____.

| red | odor | foot |

**2** _____ helps us hide our natural body odor.

| dogs | deodorant | cheese |

**3** Use your deodorant before you get _____.

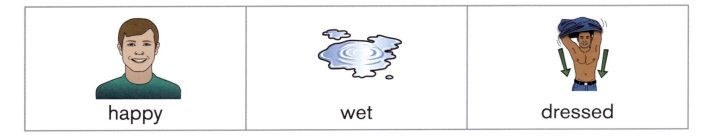

| happy | wet | dressed |

# CHAPTER 3

# Caring for Your Face and Skin

Washing Your Face

Caring for Your Skin

Treating Acne

*Products that help you take good care of your face include a scrub and a bar of soap.*

*Your face is the first thing others see of you, so make a good impression.*

# Washing Your Face

*Supplies for washing your face.*

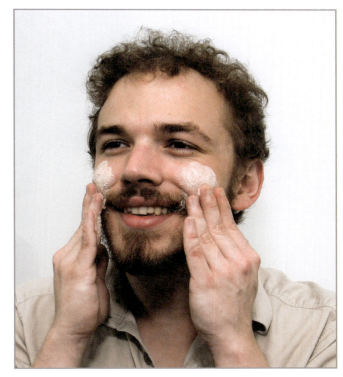

*Use a good cleanser to keep your face soft and clean.*

# Vocabulary

| | | | |
|---|---|---|---|
| 1 | wash | | to clean with water |
| 2 | depend | | to rely on for support |
| 3 | active | | being in motion, doing things |
| 4 | problem | | an issue you must deal with |
| 5 | scalding | | burning yourself with something, like a hot liquid |
| 6 | moisturizer | | a lotion that prevents dry skin |

Your face is the first thing people see of you.

And some days you may need to **wash** it more than

once. It **depends** on what you do during the day. The

more **active** you are, the more often you may need to

wash. But make sure not to wash your face too often or

it will dry your skin. Use a **moisturizer** if dry skin is a

**problem** for you.

# Step by Step

**1** Gather supplies to wash your face.

**2** Turn faucets on and test the temperature.

**3** Get hands wet . . .

**4** . . . and moisten your face.

**5** Lather soap on your hands under the faucet.

**6** Cover face with soap, keeping eyes closed.

**7** Get hands wet again . . .

**8** . . . and wash soap off face.

**9** Turn off the water.

**10** Dry face with a towel.

**11** Hang up the towel.

Turn on cold water and slowly add hot water to

avoid **scalding**. Practice this with different kinds of faucets.

Get the kind of soap you prefer, like liquid or bar soap.

Some people have dry facial skin during winter. Use a

**moisturizer** if that is a problem for you.

# Problem Solving

**1** The water is too hot for washing your face. What do you do?

_____

_____

_____

**2** Your face feels dry and it is peeling. What do you do?

_____

_____

_____

**3** You are in a public restroom and need to wash your face. What do you do?

_____

_____

_____

# Quiz

**1**

Your _____ is the first thing people see.

| | | |
|---|---|---|
|  |  | |
| car | face | mouse |

**2**

Some days you need to wash your face more than ___.

| | | |
|---|---|---|
| **2** | **1** |  |
| twice | once | turtle |

**3**

The more active you are, the more often you need to ____.

| | | |
|---|---|---|
|  |  |  |
| wash | sing | house |

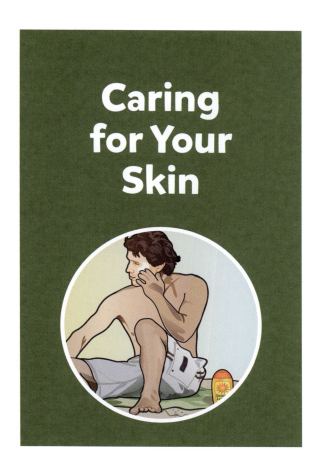

# Caring for Your Skin

*Supplies for keeping your skin protected.*

*Using sunscreens and wearing hats help you avoid sunburn and prevent wrinkles.*

# Vocabulary

| | | | |
|---|---|---|---|
| 1 | protect | | to keep safe from harm |
| 2 | sunscreen | | a lotion that protects skin from sunlight |
| 3 | wrinkles | | lines in the skin from aging, or stress, or too much sun |
| 4 | manage | | to exert control over something |
| 5 | stress | | having a lot of pressure or strain over something |
| 6 | excess | | having too much of something |

**Protect** yourself from sunburn by using **sunscreen**

and protective clothing. Do not smoke. It gives you

**wrinkles**. Follow a healthy diet. What you eat affects your

skin. And **manage** your **stress**. When you are worried, it

can make you look older than you are. And stress can

also cause acne.

# Step by Step

**1** Use sunscreen on your face.

**2** Wear clothing and hats that protect from the sun.

**3** Eat healthy.

**4** Manage stress.

**5** *Use a moisturizer to avoid dry skin.*

**6** *Avoid harsh soaps.*

Limit your bath time. **Excess** bathing can cause

dry facial skin. Stay away from strong soaps. They can

take healthy oils out of your facial skin. Pat yourself dry

with a towel after bathing so some moisture stays on your

face. And use a moisturizer to avoid dry facial skin.

# Problem Solving

**1** You like sunbathing but it gives you skin wrinkles. What should you do?

_____

_____

_____

**2** You like fast foods but are having a problem with dry skin. What can you do?

_____

_____

_____

**3** You have a lot of stress and it makes you look older. What can you do?

_____

_____

_____

# Quiz

**1**

Protect yourself from the sun by using _____.

|  |  |  |
|:---:|:---:|:---:|
| sugar | sunscreen | napkin |

**2**

Follow a healthy _____.

|  |  |  |
|:---:|:---:|:---:|
| diet | cat | cotton |

**3**

Manage your _____.

|  |  |  |
|:---:|:---:|:---:|
| goat | orange | stress |

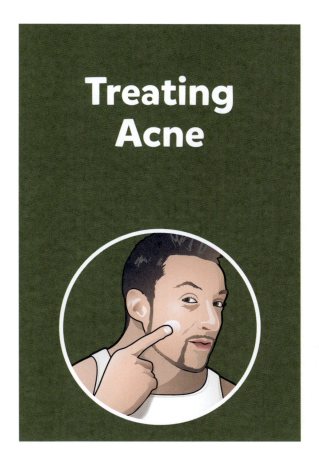

# Treating Acne

*Supplies for treating acne.*

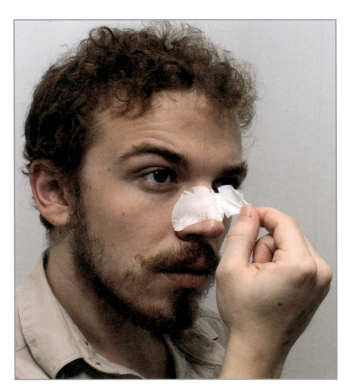

*Apply commercial treatments to deal with acne.*

# Vocabulary

| | | | |
|---|---|---|---|
| 1 | acne | | a common skin disease |
| 2 | common | | widely known or not unusual |
| 3 | embarrassed | | to feel ill at ease |
| 4 | important | | something of great value |
| 5 | treatment | | medical care given to patients |
| 6 | recommend | | to advise or suggest something |

**Acne** is **common** among young people. But it still

can be **embarrassing**. So finding a way to deal with it

is **important**. Do not try to scrub or wash it away. That

only makes it worse. Cleansing your skin once a day with

a **treatment** **recommended** by your doctor can help clear it

up.

**1** Supplies for acne treatment.

**2** Wash and dry your face.

**3** Take the cap off the tube.

**4** Squeeze a small amount in your hand and dab on your face.

5 *Wash your hands.*

6 *Put the tube away.*

Use only gentle products for facial **acne**. Not like

those you may use for the rest of your body. Do not

try to cure acne by drying out your skin. Keep your hair

out of your face to prevent forehead acne. Keep your skin

moisturized. If you use a stronger acne product, just dab

at each pimple. Do not put it all over your face.

# Problem Solving

**1** Who can you ask about what to do with your acne? Who can you talk to?

_____

_____

_____

**2** You are unsure about which anti-acne product to buy. What should you do?

_____

_____

_____

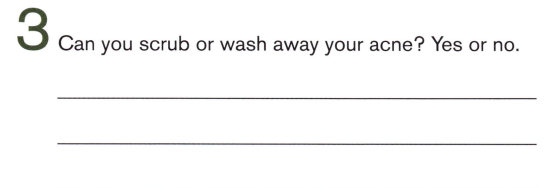

**3** Can you scrub or wash away your acne? Yes or no.

_____

_____

_____

# Quiz

**1**  _____ is common among young people.

| | | |
|---|---|---|
| money | milk | acne |

**2**  Acne can be very _____.

| | | |
|---|---|---|
| black | common | table |

**3** Cleanse daily with a treatment recommended by your _____.

| | | |
|---|---|---|
| teacher | doctor | mom |

# CHAPTER 4

# Caring for Your Hair

**Washing Your Hair**

**Combing and Brushing Hair**

**Styling Your Hair**

*Wet your hair before shampooing it . . .*

*. . . then rub the shampoo into your scalp evenly.*

# Washing Your Hair

Supplies for washing your hair.

Lather in the shampoo until it covers your scalp.

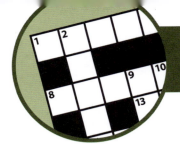
| 1 | product | | something commercial created by effort |
|---|---|---|---|
| 2 | damage | | harm to somebody or something |
| 3 | over wash | | washing your hair too often, or with too much shampoo |
| 4 | avoid | | to keep away from somebody or something |
| 5 | shampoo | | a product used to wash hair |
| 6 | conditioner | | hair care product for washing hair |

Wash your hair at least every other day. Or every

day. Try not to **over wash** your hair. But know that it is

not necessary to wash your hair every day. If you have

to, it might be because you are using the wrong hair

**products**. After showering, first shake out extra water in

your hair. And **avoid** showering or bathing in hot water.

That can lose valuable hair oils.

**1** Gather supplies.

**2** In the shower, wet your hair.

**3** Put some shampoo in the palm of your hand.

**4** Lather the shampoo into your hair with your fingers.

**5** Rinse out the shampoo.

**6** Put some conditioner in the palm of your hand.

 **7** *Let the conditioner stay in your hair for a few minutes.*

**8** *Rinse out the conditioner.*

**9** *Dry your hair with a towel.*

If you dye your hair often, it can dry out and

**damage** your hair. What you eat is also important. Your

diet choices affect the quality of your hair. Use **conditioners**

along with **shampoos** to wash your hair. But be careful to

use hair **products** that are not harmful. Get regular haircuts

to stop split ends from damaging your hair.

# Problem Solving

**1** You do not know how often to wash your hair. What should you do?

_____

_____

_____

**2** You cannot remember the difference between shampoo and conditioner. What can you do?

_____

_____

_____

**3** You think your shampoo is making your scalp itch. What should you do?

_____

_____

_____

# Quiz

**1** Wash your hair at least every other ____.

| | | |
|---|---|---|
|  |  |  |
| bug | month | day |

**2** Be careful to use ____ ____ that aren't harmful.

| | | |
|---|---|---|
|  |  |  |
| dog foods | hair products | birthday cakes |

**3** Use conditioners along with ____.

| | | |
|---|---|---|
|  |  |  |
| mustard | shampoo | cheese |

# Combing and Brushing Hair

*Supplies for combing and brushing hair.*

*After washing and drying your hair, brush or comb in your style.*

| | | | |
|---|---|---|---|
| 1 | comb | | a tool for combing your hair |
| 2 | brush | | a tool with bristles and a handle for combing your hair |
| 3 | hairstyle | | how you choose to wear your hair |
| 4 | thick | | a deep or heavy mass |
| 5 | gently | | to do something slowly or smoothly |
| 6 | tangles | | when something gets messed up, like your hair can get |

How much time you need to **comb** or **brush** your

hair depends on how long it is. What **hairstyle** you have.

And how **thick** your hair is. Find the right kind of combs

or brushes for your hair. Comb **gently** or you can damage

your hair. Do not comb too often. And keep your combs

and brushes clean.

# Step by Step

**1** Get supplies for combing or brushing hair.

**2** Comb or brush in front of a well-lit mirror.

**3** Gently comb out the tangles.

**4** Part hair neatly.

**5** Brush gently.

**6** Use hair gel if you like.

**7** Use a pick for hard-to-comb hair.

**8** Remove hair from combs and brushes.

**9** Put supplies away.

Make sure your hair is partially dry before you

**comb** or **brush** it. Then comb out any **tangles**. Part your

hair from back to front. Start at the roots and **brush**

through to the tip of your hair. Take your comb and brush

with you when you leave home. You may need them.

# Problem Solving

**1** Your hair is long and tangled. How should you take care of it?

_____

_____

_____

**2** You do not have time to brush carefully. What should you do?

_____

_____

_____

**3** Your brush is full of hair and it is hard to use it. What should you do?

_____

_____

_____

# Quiz

**1**  It takes longer to comb long ____.

| | | |
|---|---|---|
| lemon | hair | cat |

**2**    Select combs and brushes that ____ best for you.

| | | |
|---|---|---|
| dance | work | sit |

**3**   Use a comb to comb out ____.

| | | |
|---|---|---|
| melons | tangles | chairs |

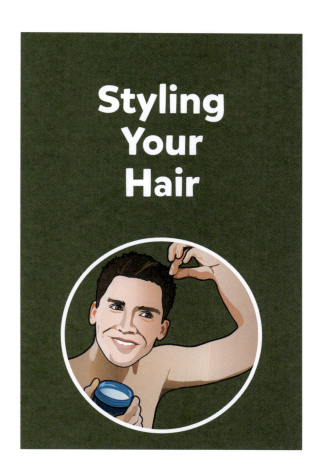

# Styling Your Hair

*Supplies for styling your hair.*

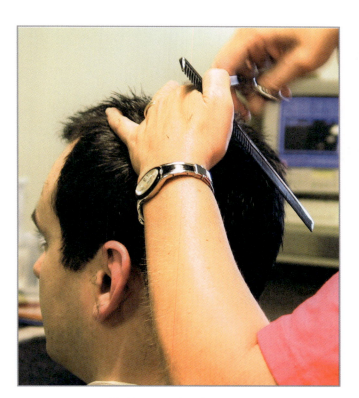

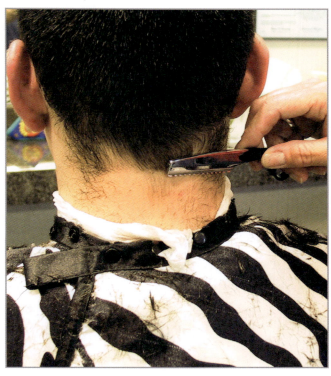

*Tell your barber what style of hair you like before he starts cutting.*

# Vocabulary

| 1 | hairstyle | | how you choose to wear your hair |
|---|---|---|---|
| 2 | personality | | the things that make you who you are |
| 3 | magazine | | a published collection of stories and pictures |
| 4 | barber | | a person who cuts hair |
| 5 | appeal | | something that you like |
| 6 | extreme | | something that goes beyond normal |

There are many male **hairstyles** to choose from.

The style you choose says a lot about who you are.

Finding one that fits your **personality** is important. Think

about a style you like. Look through **magazines** to see

which style **appeals** to you. And show it to your **barber**.

# Steps to Perform

**1** *Hairstyles differ, from informal . . .*

**2** *. . . to more traditionally formal.*

**3** *It's your choice . . .*

**4** *. . . what style you like.*

**5** *More traditional . . .*

**6** *. . . less traditional.*

**7** *Most men don't dye their hair . . .*

**8** *. . . but some do. It's your choice.*

**9** *Spiked hair is extreme but popular . . .*

**10** *. . . but mohawks are not in style. Still, it's your choice.*

**11** *Whatever style you choose . . .*

**12** *. . . remember that you're the one who has to live with it.*

**Styling Your Hair    143**

# Helpful Tips

There may be some **hairstyles** that you like but

that do not fit your **personality**. Or they may be too

**extreme** for others, such as the people you work with. But

that is your choice to make. Whatever hairstyle you choose,

you must be ready to live with it.

# Problem Solving

**1** You are not sure how to choose a hairstyle for yourself. What should you do?

_____

_____

_____

**2** You think the hairstyle you like is too extreme. What should you do?

_____

_____

_____

**3** Your barber does not have any hairstyle ideas for you. What should you do?

_____

_____

_____

# Quiz

**1**  There are many male _____ to choose from.

| | | |
|---|---|---|
|  chairs |  styles |  tomatoes |

**2**  Finding one that fits your _____ is important.

| | | |
|---|---|---|
|  car |  personality | apple |

**3**  Look through _____ to find a hairstyle you like.

| | | |
|---|---|---|
|  school |  grass |  magazines |

# Dressing for Success

Dressing for an Event

Dressing for the Weather

Buying Clothes

Choosing Daily Outfits

Having Your Own Personal Style

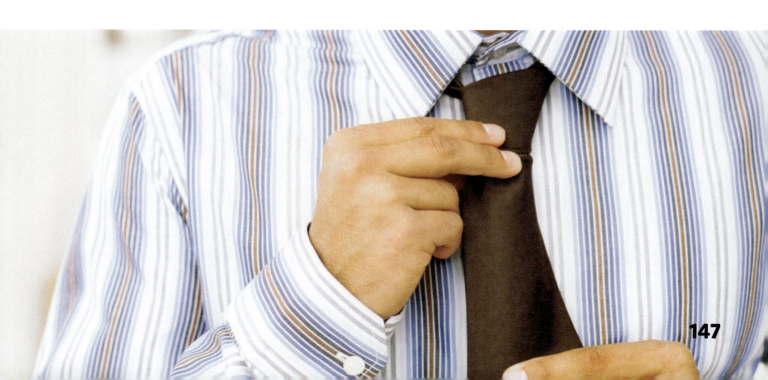

*Take your time when picking out new clothes . . .*

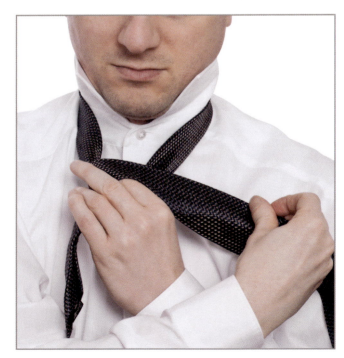

*. . . because what you wear says a lot about who you are.*

# Dressing for an Event

*A selection of ties to be worn to formal events.*

*For every event, there is a way to dress appropriately.*

# Vocabulary

| | | | |
|---|---|---|---|
| 1 | event | | a social gathering or activity |
| 2 | style | | a distinct appearance |
| 3 | formal dress | | dressing up for a formal occasion |
| 4 | casual dress | | dressing down for a casual occasion |
| 5 | magazine | | a published collection of stories and pictures |
| 6 | underwear | | clothes worn under pants |

For every kind of activity or **event**, there is a

right way to dress. Dressing the right way for an activity

is called **style**. You dress in a **formal** style if you are

going to a wedding. You dress in a more **casual** style for

a sports event. Dressing in the proper style for the event

is an important skill.

*Dress formally for formal events, like a wedding.*

*Dress casually for casual occasions, like a sports event.*

Be aware of how others dress for different kinds

of **events**. Look at **magazines** to see how others dress

for certain events. Find examples of **formal dress** and

**casual dress** and study them. Ask for advice from others.

Find out how everything you wear needs to go together.

Even shoes and socks and **underwear**.

# Problem Solving

**1** You don't get what style means. What should you do?

_____

_____

_____

**2** You don't have any formal dress clothes. What should you do?

_____

_____

_____

**3** The clothes you picked out don't go together. What should you do?

_____

_____

_____

# Quiz

**1** For every activity, there is a right way to _____.

| | | |
|:---:|:---:|:---:|
|  | | |
| dress | cook | purple |

**2** Dressing the right way is called _____.

| | | |
|:---:|:---:|:---:|
|  | | |
| chicken | style | soup |

**3** You dress for a sports event in a _____ style.

| | | |
|:---:|:---:|:---:|
| 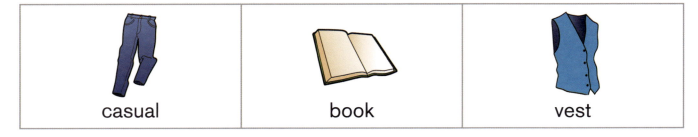 | | |
| casual | book | vest |

# Dressing for the Weather

*Dress appropriately for the weather.*

*Be ready for it, whatever the weather.*

# Vocabulary

| | | | |
|---|---|---|---|
| 1 | layers | | wearing many thin clothing items for cold weather |
| 2 | weather | | the action of outdoor elements like heat and cold |
| 3 | spikes | | spiked shoe pull-ons to prevent icy winter falls |
| 4 | lightweight | | clothing that is light, not heavy |
| 5 | fabrics | | cloth, another word for clothes |
| 6 | loose-fitting | | clothes that are loose, not tight |

Dress in **layers** when dressing for cold **weather**.

Put on many thin layers instead of a few thick layers. It

will insulate you better and, if it gets warmer, you can

take some off. Wear raincoats and take an umbrella when

it rains. Wear light colors and **lightweight fabrics** when it

is hot, and shorts if it is really hot.

# Steps to Perform

## When it is Cold

**1** Check the weather report before going out.

**2** Get your winter coat . . .

**3** . . . and your winter hat . . .

**4** . . . and your winter gloves . . .

**5** . . . and a scarf.

**6** Put on winter boots.

# Steps to Perform

## When it is Hot

**7** *Dress for warm or hot weather.*

**8** *Wear a cap if the sun is out . . .*

## When it is Raining

**9** *. . . a raincoat when it pours . . .*

**10** *. . . and carry an umbrella.*

**11** *Wear rain boots to keep your feet dry.*

Extremities like hands, head, and feet are the

places on your body that tend to get the coldest. So

when it is cold, remember to wear hats and gloves. In

the winter, you can also wear boots or **spiked** pull-ons

over your shoes to avoid falls when it is icy. Wear

**loose-fitting** clothes when it's hot.

# Problem Solving

**1** The weather report is for a cold day tomorrow.
How should you dress?

_____

_____

_____

**2** The weather report is for a hot day tomorrow.
How should you dress?

_____

_____

_____

**3** The weather report is for rain tomorrow.
How should you dress?

_____

_____

_____

# Quiz

**1**

Dress   in   layers   for   cold   _____.

|  |  |  |
|---|---|---|
| snow | weather | cereal |

**2**

Put   on   many   thin   _____.

|  |  |  |
|---|---|---|
| layers | mice | cookies |

**3**

Wear   light   _____   when   it   is   hot.

|  |  |  |
|---|---|---|
| dogs | feathers | clothing |

# Buying Clothes

*You will have many clothes choices to make.*

*Take your time buying clothes to get what you really want and need.*

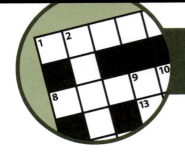
| | | | |
|---|---|---|---|
| **1** | internet | | a worldwide computer network |
| **2** | immediate | | right away, now |
| **3** | matching | | things that go together |
| **4** | graduation | | a diploma ceremony when you finish school |
| **5** | expensive | | costs a lot |
| **6** | discount | | a deduction for buyers off the usual cost of an item |

Start by planning ahead. Look through magazines

and on the **internet**. That will give you some idea of what

you want to look for. Consider if you have **immediate**

needs? Like for a party or **graduation**? And think about

**matching** clothes. If you buy a new shirt, do you have

pants that go with it? Shoes that go with it? Socks?

A jacket?

# Step by Step

**1** *When shopping for clothes, know your size.*

**2** *Don't hesitate to ask questions.*

**3** *Try on new clothes in the dressing rooms.*

**4** *Look for an empty stall.*

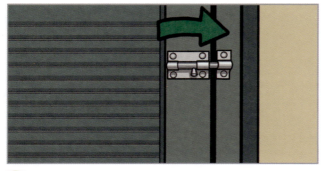

**5** *Lock door from inside.*

**6** *Put clothes back on rack.*

**7** *Try on new clothes.*

**8** *Look in a mirror to see how it looks.*

**9** *Put your clothes back on.*

**10** *Return clothes to where you got them . . .*

**11** *. . . or give them to staff.*

Clothes can be **expensive**. One tip for buying new

clothes that are **discounted** is to buy them out of season.

Buy sweaters in the summer and shorts in the winter. First

make a clothes budget and then make a list of clothes

you want. That way you will know what you can afford.

And look for discount stores. You can do that online.

# Problem Solving

**1** You do not know where to shop or what to buy. What can you do?

_____

_____

_____

**2** You do not have the clothes for matching outfits.
What do you need to do?

_____

_____

_____

**3** You do not know where to buy clothes at a discount.
What should you do?

_____

_____

_____

# Quiz

**1**  To find clothes you might want to buy, look through a____.

| | | |
|---|---|---|
|  |  |  |
| car | magazine | book |

**2** If you buy a shirt, do you have ____ that go with it?

| | | |
|---|---|---|
|  |  |  |
| candy | pants | rain |

**3**   Clothes that go together are called ____.

| | | |
|---|---|---|
|  | |  |
| outfits | elephants | alphabet |

# Choosing Daily Outfits

*Pick a color that looks good on you.*

*When choosing outfits, look for clothes that match.*

# Vocabulary

| | | | |
|---|---|---|---|
| 1 | daily |  | every day |
| 2 | outfit | | a set of clothes that go together |
| 3 | build | | to make something |
| 4 | dressing room | | a room to try on new clothes |
| 5 | salesperson | | someone who helps you find what you want |
| 6 | basic | | simple, not complicated |

To choose a **daily outfit**, you have to match all

the clothes you are wearing. But most important is being

able to match shirts with pants. The best way to match is

by color, like blue jeans with a shirt of any color. Most

shirts of any color will go well with blue jeans. Or with

black pants. You can **build** an outfit from that.

*Match shirts with pants and build outfits based on those colors.*

*Try on pants and a shirt in the store's dressing room.*

*If you're not sure about something, ask a friend or a salesperson.*

# Helpful Tips

Spend some time looking in the **dressing room**

mirror when you buy clothes. See if the **outfit** you want

to buy matches. If you are not sure, ask someone else

how it looks. You can either ask a friend or the store

**salesperson**. If you **build** most of your outfits from **basic**

colors, you will always have matching clothes.

# Problem Solving

**1** You are not sure you can find clothes that match. What can you do?

_____

_____

_____

**2** You like colorful clothes but have trouble matching them. What should you do?

_____

_____

_____

**3** You cannot find a salesperson at the store. What should you do?

_____

_____

_____

# Quiz

**1** To find an outfit, you have to match all your _____.

| | | |
|---|---|---|
|  |  |  |
| clothes | chickens | pencils |

**2** It is important to match shirts with _____.

| | | |
|---|---|---|
|  |  |  |
| apples | pants | turkeys |

**3** Most shirts will look good with _____ _____.

| | | |
|---|---|---|
|  |  |  |
| jogging suits | blue jeans | french fries |

# Having Your Own Personal Style

*How you choose to dress is your personal style.*

*There are as many personal styles as there are people. Find what works for you.*

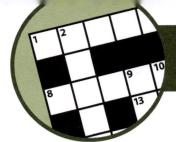

# Vocabulary

| 1 | personal style | | how you present yourself and what things you like |
|---|---|---|---|
| 2 | country music | | a form of music that comes from the South |
| 3 | express | | how you present yourself |
| 4 | extreme | | something that is over the top, too much |
| 5 | tattooing | | an inking process that puts permanent patterns on your body |
| 6 | piercing | | making small holes in body parts, such as ears or nose, to wear jewelry |

You know who you are and what you like.

Dressing to fit your **personal** **style** helps you be yourself.

Consider the styles you like, to see how to **express**

yourself. For example, jeans and cowboy shirts are your

style if you like **country** **music**. Beware of **extreme** styles

like **tattooing** and **piercing**. You have to live with them.

*Your personal style says a lot about who you are.*

*Beware of extreme decorations that you may have to live with for a long time.*

Everyone has a **personal style**. What is yours?

Think about the things you like. They are a clue to

your style. Are you a sports fan? A music fan? Which

celebrities do you like? You might want to dress a little

like those you admire. But do it your way. Be yourself.

Being original is the key.

# Problem Solving

**1** You are already happy with your personal style. What should you do?

_____

_____

_____

**2** You do not know how to express your personal style. What can you do?

_____

_____

_____

**3** You want to get a tattoo. What should you do?

_____

_____

_____

# Quiz

**1**   Dressing to fit your personal style helps you be ____.

|  |  |  |
|:---:|:---:|:---:|
| sad | truck | yourself |

**2**    Consider styles you like, to decide how to ____ yourself.

|  |  |  |
|:---:|:---:|:---:|
| banana | present | paper |

**3**  Beware of extreme ____.

|  |  |  |
|:---:|:---:|:---:|
| styles | weather | chocolate |

# CHAPTER 6

# Other Personal Care Issues

Keeping Your Hands Clean

Caring for Your Nails

Checking Yourself Over

*No act of personal care is more important than keeping your hands clean.*

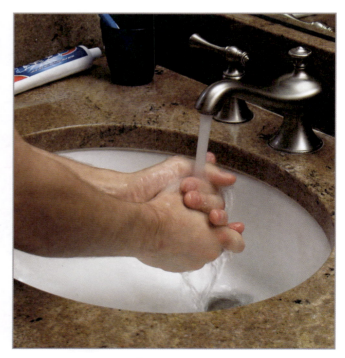

*Wash your hands with hand soap or a sanitizer like Purell® to keep them clean.*

# Keeping Your Hands Clean

*Supplies for keeping your hands clean.*

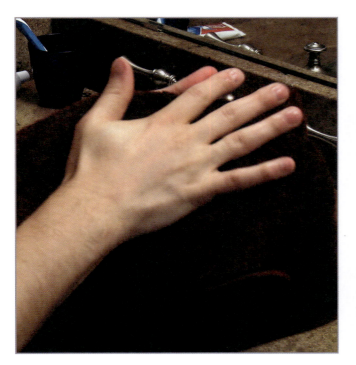

*Keeping your hands clean helps prevent illness.*

# Vocabulary

| | | | |
|---|---|---|---|
| 1 | touch | | when you contact someone else |
| 2 | important | | something of great value |
| 3 | surface | | the top or outer part of something |
| 4 | handle | | the part of a thing you hold to when carrying it |
| 5 | coughing | | a sudden, noisy expulsion of sound from the mouth |
| 6 | sneezing | | noisy sound of air coming out of your nose |

A simple **touch** can spread an illness. So keeping

your hands clean throughout the day is **important**. Clean

your hands before and after **handling** or preparing food.

Clean hands before and after eating. Also before and after

being around someone who is sick. And when putting in

or taking out contact lenses.

# Step by Step

**1** Gather supplies.

**2** Turn on faucet and find the right temperature.

**3** Get your hands wet.

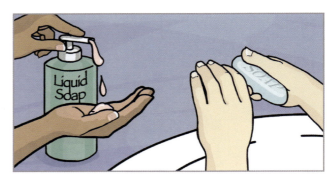

**4** Apply soap.

**5** Lather your hands.

**6** Scrub your hands with brush.

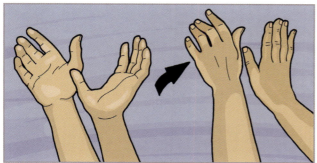

**7** *Check both sides to make sure hands are clean.*

**8** *Turn faucet off.*

**9** *Dry hands with towel.*

**10** *Dry hands in restroom with dryer or paper towels.*

Clean your hands after using the toilet. After

wiping or blowing your nose. After **coughing** or **sneezing**.

After changing diapers. And after **touching** common **surfaces**

like **handles** or door knobs. You can use any kind

of soap.

**1** Your friend is sick when you visit him. What should you do after you leave?

_____

_____

_____

**2** You are helping prepare supper. What should you do first?

_____

_____

_____

**3** You are going to take off your contact lenses. What should you do first?

_____

_____

_____

# Quiz

**1**  A simple touch can spread an ____.

| | | |
|---|---|---|
| apple | illness | idea |

**2**  Keeping your hands clean is ____.

| | | |
|---|---|---|
| sad | important | bat |

**3**   Clean your hands before handling or preparing ____.

| | | |
|---|---|---|
| food | money | flowers |

# Caring for Your Nails

*Fingernail and toenail clippers.*

*Be careful when clipping nails.*

# Vocabulary

| | | | |
|---|---|---|---|
| 1 | moisturizer | | a lotion that prevents dryness |
| 2 | trim | | to make neat by clipping |
| 3 | clipper | | a tool that cuts or trims |
| 4 | toenails | | the nail at the end of a toe |
| 5 | fingernails | | the nail at the end of a finger |
| 6 | ingrown nails | | a nail that has grown into the skin |

It is a good idea to **trim** your nails every

week. Both **toenails** and **fingernails** need weekly care. But

sometimes nails break and need care right away. Make

sure you always have nail **clippers** for both toenails and

fingernails.

# Step by Step

**1** Get fingernail clippers.

**2** Wash hands. Scrub nails, if necessary, with a brush.

**3** Clip each nail from right to left . . .

**4** . . . then from left to right.

**5** Sit down to reach toenails.

**6** Clip from right to left . . .

*. . . then from left to right.*

**7**

*Toss nails into the trash.*

**8**

*Put clippers back.*

**9**

It is easy to hurt yourself when **trimming** nails.

Trim carefully after taking a shower or any time when nails

are soft and easy to work with. You can also use hand

and foot **moisturizers** if you want. See your doctor for

**ingrown toenails** and any other nail problems.

# Problem Solving

**1** You forgot to trim your nails last week. What can you do?

_____

_____

_____

**2** You have clippers for toenails but not fingernails. What should you do?

_____

_____

_____

**3** You have an ingrown toenail. What do you do?

_____

_____

_____

**1**   Trim   your   nails   every   _____.

|  |  |  |
|---|---|---|
| week | mountain | lips |

**2**   Trim   _____   right   away   when   they   break.

|  | |  |
|---|---|---|
| pumpkins | nails | hamsters |

**3**   Be   sure   you   have   nail   _____   around.

|  |  |  |
|---|---|---|
| pineapple | clippers | fish |

# Checking Yourself Over

*Take a close look in the mirror before you leave home . . .*

*. . . and make sure you are looking good.*

# Vocabulary

| | | | |
|---|---|---|---|
| 1 | usually | | something that happens most of the time, but not all the time |
| 2 | everything | | all things or all of a group of things |
| 3 | identification card | | a card with your picture that proves who you are |
| 4 | correcting | | making free from error |
| 5 | zipper | | metal or plastic teeth that close pants or jackets |
| 6 | neat | | in order, clean |

Once you leave home for the day, it is **usually**

hard to go back. So make sure you look good and have

**everything** you need before you go. Are you dressed for

the weather? Do you have a wallet with some money and

an **identification card**? Then take one last look in the

mirror to see if you look okay.

# Step by Step

**1** *Check yourself over before leaving home.*

**2** *Is your hair okay?*

**3** *Remember to clean glasses.*

**4** *Is your face clean?*

**5** *Do you need to blow your nose?*

**6** *Are your hands and fingernails clean?*

**7** Make sure your buttons are buttoned.

**8** Tuck your shirt in.

**9** Zip up your pants.

**10** Buckle your belt and tie your shoes.

**11** Take one last look in the mirror.

# Helpful Tips

Before you leave home, see if there are any

problems that need **correcting**. Is your hair in place?

Are your glasses clean? How about hands and fingernails?

Are buttons and **zippers** closed? Are shoes tied and **neat**?

Do you have **everything** you need?

# Problem Solving

**1** You have left home but forgot something. What should you do?

_____

_____

_____

**2** You left home but are not dressed for the weather. What should you do?

_____

_____

_____

**3** You do not have an identification card. What should you do?

_____

_____

_____

# Quiz

**1**
Once you leave home, you cannot easily ____ ____.

| go back | jump up | go down |

**2**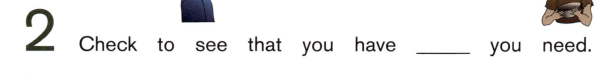
Check to see that you have ____ you need.

| chair | everything | apple |

**3**
Take one last look in the ____.

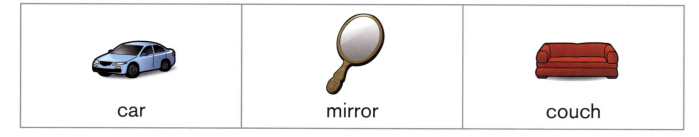

| car | mirror | couch |

# CHAPTER 7

# Caring for Your Eyes

Taking Care of Your Glasses

Taking Care of Your Contacts

Being Aware of Eye Safety

Going to the Optometrist

*Make sure you have a glass cleaner and a soft cloth at hand.*

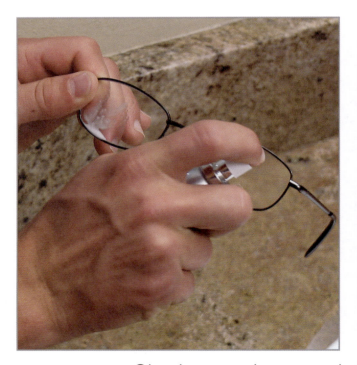

*Cleaning your glasses regularly is key to good, clear vision.*

# Taking Care of Your Glasses

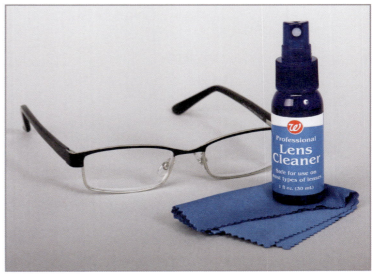

*Eye glass cleaner and soft cloth.*

*Take good care of your glasses.*

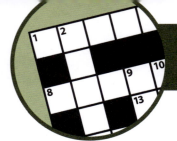

# Vocabulary

| | | | |
|---|---|---|---|
| 1 | vision | | how you see things |
| 2 | attractive | | pleasing to the eye or mind |
| 3 | lint-free cloth | | for cleaning glasses |
| 4 | scratching | | to make a surface mark with a sharp object |
| 5 | surface | | the top or outer part of something |
| 6 | lenses | | glasses you see through |

If you need glasses, it is likely you wear them

most of the time. So you want them to do their job

and give you clear **vision**. Also, you want them to be

**attractive**. When you select new glasses, ask for help to

find a pair you really like. Use glass spray and a

**lint-free cloth** to keep them clean.

# Steps to Perform

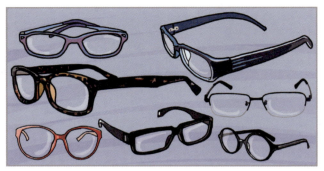

1 Pick out glasses you like.

2 Clean with lint-free cloth.

3 Always store in case.

4 Use two hands to put on and take off.

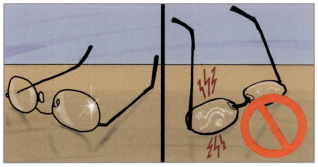

**5** *Don't set glasses down on hard surfaces.*

**6** *Be careful where you put your glasses.*

Keeping your glasses in their case when not in

use protects them from **scratching**. Putting the **lenses** face

down on a hard **surface** can also scratch them. Use two

hands when putting glasses on. That helps keep them from

bending.

# Problem Solving

**1** You're not sure which glasses to buy. Who can you ask?

_____

_____

_____

**2** You keep scratching your glasses. What can you do to prevent it?

_____

_____

_____

**3** Your glasses aren't clean and you can't see. What should you do?

_____

_____

_____

# Quiz

**1**  Glasses give you clear _____.

|  |  |  |
|:---:|:---:|:---:|
| bananas | books | vision |

**2** And you want them to be _____.

|  |  |  |
|:---:|:---:|:---:|
| blue | happy | attractive |

**3** Use a spray and lint-free _____ to clean them.

| 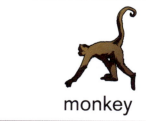 |  |  |
|:---:|:---:|:---:|
| monkey | cloth | table |

# Taking Care of Your Contacts

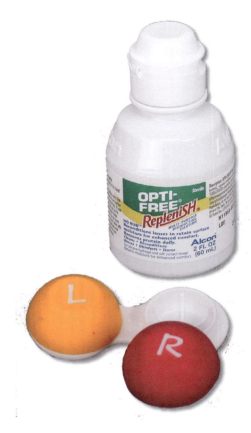

*Contact supplies.*

*Open contact container and wash hands with a non-cosmetic soap before putting in contacts.*

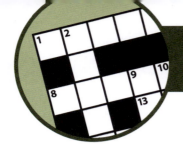

# Vocabulary

| | | | |
|---|---|---|---|
| **1** | contacts | | lenses you put over your eyes |
| **2** | optometrist | | a doctor who treats eyes |
| **3** | disposable | | something you can throw away |
| **4** | non-cosmetic soap | | a soap that is safe for your eyes |
| **5** | infection | | an invasion of the body by germs that can make you sick |
| **6** | sensitive | | a strong response to a condition |

**Contacts** can be hard to put in at first. Ask your

**optometrist** to show you how to put them in. And ask

for daily **disposable** lenses. They need less care than other

lenses. Wash and rinse your hands using a **non-cosmetic**

**soap** before you put your contacts in your eyes.

**1** Wash and dry your hands well.

**2** Remove lens from the case.

**3** Pour cleaning solution over lens in palm of your hand.

**4** Repeat for second eye.

**5** *Inspect each contact lens for dirt or dust.*

**6** *Holding your eyelids open, insert a contact.*

**7** *To remove, gently pinch the lens.*

**8** *Place lens in case and cover with lens solution.*

Don't wear another person's **contacts**. It can give

you an eye **infection**. Do not sleep with contacts in your

eyes unless you have extended-care lenses. Make sure you

have special eye drops just for contacts. Contacts can

make your eyes **sensitive** to sunlight. Consider getting

sunglasses.

# Problem Solving

**1** You find contacts very hard to put in. Who can help you learn how?

_____

_____

_____

**2** You're thinking about borrowing your friend's contacts. Should you?

_____

_____

_____

**3** You fell asleep with your contacts on. Is that okay?

_____

_____

_____

# Quiz

**1**  _____ can be hard to put in at first.

| | | |
|---|---|---|
|  |  |  |
| clocks | candles | contacts |

**2**  Ask your _____ to show you how to put them in.

| | | |
|---|---|---|
|  |  | |
| cat | optometrist | coffee |

**3** Before putting in, wash and rinse your _____.

| | | |
|---|---|---|
|  |  |  |
| feet | hands | teeth |

# Being Aware of Eye Safety

*Safety glasses and sunglasses help protect your eyes.*

*It is important to wear safety glasses when doing some jobs.*

# Vocabulary

| | | | |
|---|---|---|---|
| 1 | safety glasses | | special glasses you use for work |
| 2 | injury | | being hurt accidentally |
| 3 | scratch | | lightly breaking your skin |
| 4 | icepack | | a cold pack to stop swelling |
| 5 | reduce | | to bring down or make less than |
| 6 | chemical | | a substance that can be dangerous |

**Safety** **glasses** prevent most types of eye **injuries**.

Wearing them on some jobs can help you keep your eyes

safe from harm. If you have already **scratched** an eye or

have been hit in your eye, call your regular doctor for

advice. But do not rub or touch your eye.

Use eye protection when doing some jobs.

Wear sunglasses and a hat to protect your eyes from the sun.

Eye protection comes in many styles, depending on the activity.

*Some professionals and athletes must use eye protection.*

Put an **icepack** on your eye to **reduce** swelling if

you have an accident and get a black eye. For other eye

**injuries**, like a **chemical** burn, you can run warm water

over your eyes to relieve the pain. But you should still

call your regular doctor. Most doctors have phone numbers

you can reach on nights and weekends.

# Problem Solving

**1** You don't have a pair of safety glasses. What should you do?

_____

_____

_____

**2** You scratched your eye at work. What should you do?

_____

_____

_____

**3** You put an icepack on to stop swelling. What else should you do?

_____

_____

_____

# Quiz

**1**  Safety _____ prevent most types of eye injuries.

| | | |
|---|---|---|
| balls | glasses | money |

**2**    If you scratch your eye, do not rub or _____ it.

| | | |
|---|---|---|
| touch | jump | sing |

**3**   If you hurt your eye accidentally, put an _____ on it.

| | | |
|---|---|---|
| ice pack | mouse | blanket |

# Going to the Optometrist

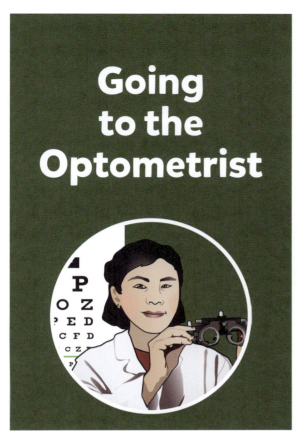

**Dr. David Park, VisionSeeUs.com**
542 Dean Street
Madison, WI 53716

Name _____

Address _____ Phone _____

City/State _____ Zip _____

| | | SPHERE | CYLINDER | AXIS | PRISM | BASE | BASE CURVE | |
|---|---|---|---|---|---|---|---|---|
| DISTANCE | M | | | | | | | ☐Plastic ☐Hi Index ☐Polycarbonate |
| | I | | | | | | | ☐Hyper Index 1.66 |
| ADD | R | | PUPIL DISTANCE PD= | | | | | |
| | L | | | | | | | |

| LENS TYPE | SEG TYPE | UV 400 Coating |
|---|---|---|
| [ ] Single Vision | [ ] Kryptok  [ ] Flat Top | [ ] Tint  [ ] SRC |

*If you think you need glasses, make an appointment with an optometrist.*

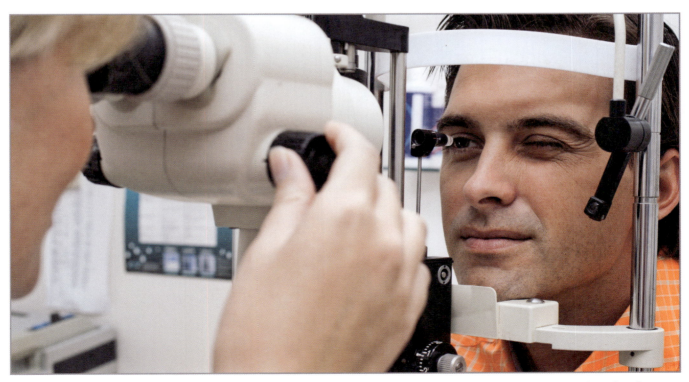

*To keep your vision intact, make regular appointments to get your eyes checked.*

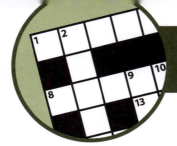

# Vocabulary

| | | | |
|---|---|---|---|
| 1 | optometrist | | an eye doctor |
| 2 | sunglasses | | dark glasses that block some sunlight |
| 3 | dilate | | when your pupils widen |
| 4 | appointment | | when you agree to meet someone |
| 5 | exam | | a test to see if things are okay |
| 6 | vision | | the ability to see |

Have regular eye **exams** to check for any

problems that may have occurred. And make sure to see

 **2**

an **optometrist** at least every two years. List questions for

you to ask the doctor before you go. Take your glasses

or contacts with you. And take **sunglasses** because your

pupils will be **dilated** when you leave.

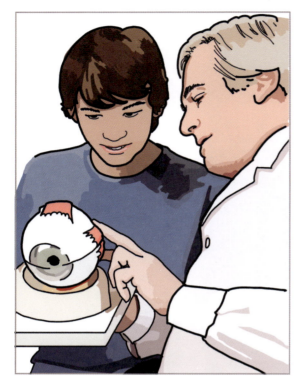

*The doctor will get close to you to look in your eyes.*

*The optometrist will tell you about your eyes.*

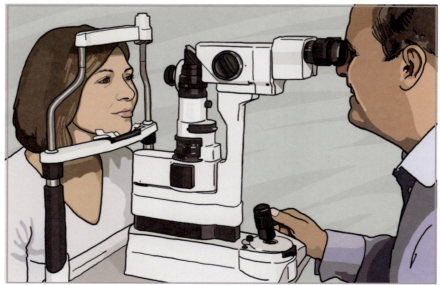

*He will examine your eyes with bright lights.*

*If you need glasses, an eye doctor can help you pick them out.*

*You may have drops put in your eyes.*

*They use special instruments to test your vision.*

**Going to the Optometrist**   **245**

# Helpful Tips

If you have a family history of eye problems, you

should see the eye doctor more often than most people.

When you make the **appointment**, say why you want to

see the **optometrist**. The **exam** will take about half an

hour. The optometrist will check your **vision** and the overall

health of your eyes.

# Problem Solving

**1** Your eyes are bothering you. What should you do?

_____

_____

_____

**2** You don't know the last time you saw your optometrist. What should you do?

_____

_____

_____

**3** You have a family history of eye problems. What can you do?

_____

_____

_____

# Quiz

**1**  Have  regular  eye  exams  to  check  for  _____.

| candy | problems | paper |
|:---:|:---:|:---:|
| candy | problems | paper |

**2**   See  an  optometrist  at  least  every  _____  years.

| **10** | **2** | **20** |
|:---:|:---:|:---:|
| ten | two | twenty |

**3**   The  doctor  will  check  your  _____.

| eyes | cats | bananas |
|:---:|:---:|:---:|
| eyes | cats | bananas |

# CHAPTER 8

# Being Social and Safe

Going Out with Friends

Getting Along with Friends

Good Touch, Bad Touch

*Nothing is more fun than going out with friends, if you make an effort to be safe.*

# Going Out with Friends

*Look good when you go out, but dress right for the occasion, whether it's formal or, as pictured here, casual.*

# Vocabulary

| | | | |
|---|---|---|---|
| **1** | extra | | more or better than ordinary |
| **2** | occasion | | an event or happening |
| **3** | formal | | being within accepted forms or expectations |
| **4** | taxi | | a paid car service that drives you somewhere |
| **5** | alcohol | | an intoxicating drink |
| **6** | drugs | | illegal chemicals that cause behavior changes |

Take **extra** care to look good before you go out.

Shower. Use deodorant. Brush your teeth. Brush or comb

your hair. Use mouthwash. Check yourself over in the mirror

before you leave. Dress nicely but dress right for the

**occasion**. Dress casually if you are going to a party with

friends. Dress formally if it is a **formal** event.

*Wear the right clothes for the occasion.*

*Check yourself in the mirror before you leave.*

*Hey, I'm looking good!*

*Stay with friends you trust.*

*Don't use alcohol or drugs!*

*Take enough money for a taxi if you need it.*

Know where you are going. Have a plan for

getting there and back. Take enough money for a **taxi** in

case you need it. Stay with friends you trust and look out

for each other. Know that you do not have to join others

who are using **alcohol** or **drugs**. Do not let anyone talk

you into doing anything you do not want to do.

# Problem Solving

**1** You are not sure how formal the event you are going to will be. What should you do?

_____

_____

_____

**2** Your friends left and you do not know how to get home. What can you do?

_____

_____

_____

**3** Your friends want you to take drugs with them. What should you do?

_____

_____

_____

# Quiz

**1**  Check yourself over in the _____ before you leave.

window

mirror

school

**2**  Dress _____ for the occasion.

wrong

right

funny

**3**  Know where you are _____ before you leave home.

singing

going

dancing

# Getting Along with Friends

*Plan things you can do together.*

*It's hard to get along with others, and takes a lot of work and understanding, but it's well worth it.*

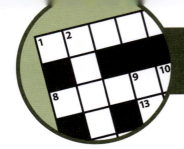

| | | | |
|---|---|---|---|
| 1 | require | | something that you have to do |
| 2 | effort | | doing something that's hard to do |
| 3 | together | | doing something with others |
| 4 | communicate | | to make known something to others |
| 5 | gently | | do something in a gradual and calm manner |
| 6 | blow up | | to explode |

To keep friends **requires** **effort** on your part. Plan

things you can do **together**. Find activities they enjoy to

share. If you go out of your way to do things they like,

they will do the same for you. **Communicate** with them.

Let them know when you are mad with them. But do it

**gently**. You may lose a friend if you **blow up** at them.

# Social Story Steps

*Be on time.*

*Mind your table manners.*

*Have fun and be a good sport.*

*Follow the rules.*

*Be there when your friends need you.*

*When you're a guest, ask what you can do.*

I broke your mug when I washed it. I'm sorry!

Well, at least you told me.

*Tell the truth, even when it's hard.*

You should wear something nicer to the restaurant.

Okay. I didn't know.

*Don't get upset when someone gives you advice.*

Learn how to compromise. Compromising is like

sharing. It means meeting your friends halfway and working

**together** to make things work. If your friends do not like

something you say or do, don't get angry with them. Talk

to them about your differences. Then if you say or do

something they don't like, they will talk with you about it.

# Problem Solving

**1** You have problems keeping friends. What can you do about it?

_____

_____

_____

**2** You sometimes get mad at your friends. What should you do?

_____

_____

_____

**3** Your friends are drinking alcohol under age. What should you do?

_____

_____

_____

**1**

Learn   how   to   _____.

|  |  |  |
|:---:|:---:|:---:|
| dance | compromise | leave |

**2**

Meet   your   _____   halfway.

|  |  |  |
|:---:|:---:|:---:|
| park | friends | school |

**3**

Talk   to   them   about   your   _____.

|  |  |  |
|:---:|:---:|:---:|
| balloons | differences | pineapple |

# Good Touch, Bad Touch

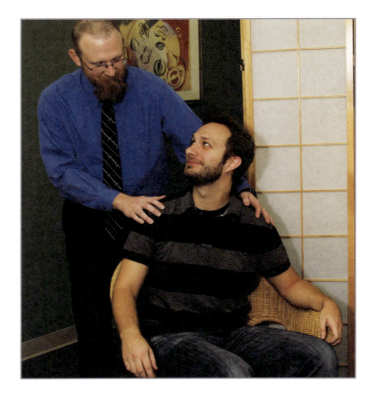

*These are good touches. But no one has the right to touch you if you don't want them to*

# Vocabulary

| | | | |
|---|---|---|---|
| 1 | right | | morally good, or acceptable |
| 2 | touch | | to make body contact with another person |
| 3 | body | | the physical part of a person, any part of your body |
| 4 | permission | | to say something is all right to say or do |
| 5 | afraid | | filled with fear |
| 6 | loud | | making a lot of noise |

No one has the **right** to **touch** any part of your

**body** unless you want them to. A bad touch is when

someone touches you without your **permission**. A good

touch is when you say it is okay to be touched. Just say

"no" or "stop" if you do not want to be touched. And if

you are **afraid**, say it **loudly** so others can hear.

## Good Touches

Sometimes teachers will touch you to give you encouragement.

*A pat on the shoulder is a gesture of congratulations.*

It's okay for a doctor to touch you during an exam.

*Friends often shake hands when they meet.*

## Bad Touches

No Touch Zone

*Some areas of your body should not be touched without your permission.*

*Sometimes people may invade your personal space.*

*If someone touches you without your permission, tell a trusted adult.*

But if someone **touches** you after you warned

them not to, then you should tell others about it. Tell

someone who has authority to do something about it. That

could be your parents. A teacher. A police officer. Or a

school counselor.

# Problem Solving

**1** You don't know if you should let someone touch you. What should you do?

_____

_____

_____

**2** You don't want someone to touch you, but you don't want to hurt their feelings. What should you do?

_____

_____

_____

**3** Someone touched you but you did not want them to. What should you do?

_____

_____

_____

# Quiz

**1**   No one can touch your body unless you ____ them to.

|  | | |
|---|---|---|
| donut | truck | want |

**2**   Bad touch is when you are touched without your ___.

| | | |
|---|---|---|
| frog | permission | table |

**3**   A good touch is when you say it is okay to be ___.

|  | | |
|---|---|---|
| sleepy | touched | hungry |

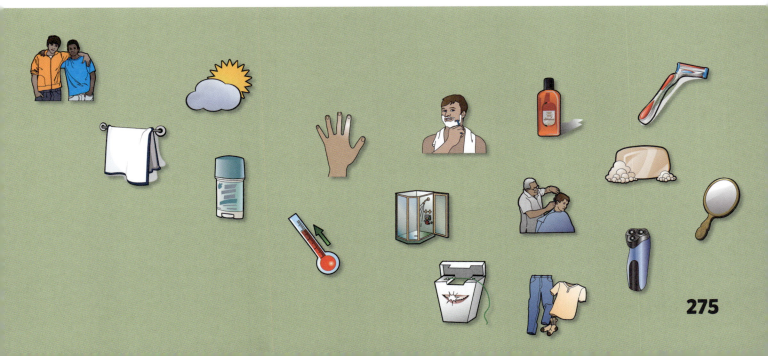

# Vocabulary Index

| Vocabulary Word | Symbol | Page |
|---|---|---|
| accident | | 80 |
| acne | | 114 |
| active | | 98 |
| afraid | | 268 |
| alcohol | | 252 |
| appeal | | 140 |
| appointment | | 242 |
| attractive | | 218 |
| avoid | | 124 |
| bacteria | | 30 |

| Vocabulary Word | Symbol | Page |
|---|---|---|
| bad breath | | 38 |
| baggy | | 80 |
| barber | | 140 |
| basic | | 174 |
| bath | | 64 |
| blades | | 72 |
| blow up | | 260 |
| body | | 268 |
| brush | | 132 |
| build | | 174 |

# Vocabulary Index

| Vocabulary Word | Symbol | Page |
|---|---|---|
| casual dress | | 150 |
| chemical | | 234 |
| clipper | | 200 |
| comb | | 132 |
| comfortable | | 30 |
| common | | 114 |
| communicate | | 260 |
| conditioner | | 124 |
| contacts | | 226 |
| correct | A+ | 14 |

| Vocabulary Word | Symbol | Page |
|---|---|---|
| correcting | | 208 |
| coughing | | 192 |
| country music | | 182 |
| blades | | 72 |
| daily | | 174 |
| damage | | 124 |
| decay | | 30 |
| dental | | 14 |
| dentist | | 46 |
| deodorant | | 88 |

# Vocabulary Index

| Vocabulary Word | Symbol | Page |
|---|---|---|
| depend | | 98 |
| dilate | | 242 |
| discount | | 166 |
| disposable | | 226 |
| disposable razor | | 80 |
| dressing room | | 174 |
| drugs | | 252 |
| effort | | 260 |
| electric razor | | 72 |
| embarrassed | | 114 |

| Vocabulary Word | Symbol | Page |
|---|---|---|
| event | | 150 |
| everything | | 208 |
| exam | | 242 |
| excess | | 106 |
| expensive | | 166 |
| explain | | 46 |
| express | | 182 |
| extra | | 252 |
| extreme | | 140 182 |
| fabrics | | 158 |

# Vocabulary Index

| Vocabulary Word | Symbol | Page |
|---|---|---|
| faucet | | 56 |
| fingernails | | 200 |
| floss | | 22 |
| fluoride | | 38 |
| force | | 38 |
| formal | | 252 |
| formal dress | | 150 |
| gently | | 132 260 |
| graduation | | 166 |
| gum line | | 22 |

| Vocabulary Word | Symbol | Page |
|---|---|---|
| gums | | 22 |
| hairstyle | | 132 140 |
| handle | | 192 |
| hygiene | | 14 |
| icepack | | 234 |
| identification card | | 208 |
| immediate | | 166 |
| important | | 114 192 |
| index finger | | 22 |
| infection | | 226 |

# Vocabulary Index

| Vocabulary Word | Symbol | Page | Vocabulary Word | Symbol | Page |
|---|---|---|---|---|---|
| ingrown nails | | 200 | loose-fitting | | 158 |
| injury | | 234 | loud | | 268 |
| insurance card | | 46 | magazine | | 140 150 |
| internet | | 166 | manage | | 106 |
| laundry | | 56 | mask | | 88 |
| layers | | 158 | matching | | 166 |
| lenses | | 218 | mirror | | 80 |
| lift | | 64 | moisturizer | | 98 200 |
| lightweight | | 158 | natural | | 88 |
| lint-free cloth | | 218 | neat | | 208 |

# Vocabulary Index

| Vocabulary Word | Symbol | Page | Vocabulary Word | Symbol | Page |
|---|---|---|---|---|---|
| nervous | | 46 | personality | | 140 |
| non-cosmetic soap | | 226 | personal style | | 182 |
| occasion | | 252 | piercing | | 182 |
| odor | | 88 | plaque | | 14 |
| option | | 30 | prefer | | 22 |
| optometrist | | 226 242 | problem | | 98 |
| outfit | | 174 | product | | 124 |
| over wash | | 124 | protect | | 106 |
| permission | | 268 | question | | 46 |
| personal | | 14 | recommend | | 114 |

# Vocabulary Index

| Vocabulary Word | Symbol | Page |
|---|---|---|
| reduce | | 234 |
| regular | | 14 |
| relax | | 46 |
| require | | 260 |
| right | | 268 |
| rinse | | 38 |
| routine | | 8 |
| rub | | 72 |
| safety glasses | | 234 |
| salesperson | | 174 |

| Vocabulary Word | Symbol | Page |
|---|---|---|
| scalding | | 98 |
| scratch | | 234 |
| scratching | | 218 |
| screen | | 72 |
| sensitive | | 30 226 |
| shampoo | | 64 124 |
| shave | | 72 80 |
| shaving lotion | | 72 |
| shower | | 56 |
| slide | | 22 |

# Vocabulary Index

# Vocabulary Index

| Vocabulary Word | Symbol | Page |
|---|---|---|
| together | | 260 |
| touch | | 192 268 |
| towel | | 56 |
| treatment | | 114 |
| trim | | 200 |
| tub | | 64 |
| underwear | | 150 |
| usually | | 208 |
| vision | | 218 242 |
| wash | | 98 |

| Vocabulary Word | Symbol | Page |
|---|---|---|
| washcloth | | 64 |
| water pick | | 30 |
| weather | | 158 |
| wrinkles | | 106 |
| zipper | | 208 |